Table of

		PAGE
☕	**INTRODUCTION**	2
⚒	**AROUND THE YARD**	3
🌳	**TREES, SHRUBS & EVERGREENS**	6
🌷	**FLOWERS**	10
🥬	**VEGETABLES**	17
🪴	**HOUSE PLANTS**	20
🦋	**PETS, PESTS & OTHER CRITTERS**	28

America's Master Gardener®

Introduction

When I was a young boy, my Grandma Puttnam introduced me to the pleasures of gardening. One of the first things she taught me was to improvise whenever and wherever I could, which meant that we'd use whatever "junk" was available – old tin cans, worn out hoses, newspaper or the like – to stop, correct, or prevent our garden growing pains.

Well, that lesson has stayed with me to this day. Wherever I go, I tell folks to reuse common household items in their garden to save time, money, and effort, and they in turn have provided me with a lot of neat ideas about how they do just that. Over the years, I've collected several thousand of these tips, tricks, and techniques, and I thought I'd share 101 of my favorite with you in this booklet.

If you need more comprehensive information, please refer to one of my other full size books:

Plants Are Still Like People; Jerry Baker's Flowering Garden; The Impatient Gardener; Fast, Easy Vegetable Garden; Jerry Baker's Lawn Book; and Happy, Healthy House Plants,

or pick up a copy of **America's Gardening Newsletter, "On The Garden Line®,"** which is also jam-packed with my timely tips, tricks, and tonics on lawn, garden, and plant care.

And if you have a question about anything related to gardening, why don't you call me **"On the Garden Line",** Saturday mornings from 8:00 a.m. - 10:00 a.m. EST on your local Mutual Broadcasting Station. The toll-free number is **1-800-634-3881.**

AROUND
The Yard

TIP #1

If your old garden hose leaks in several places, put it aside for the hot, dry summer days. Cut it in several new places, plug the one end and attach it to a faucet. It makes an excellent lawn sprinkler.

TIP #2

To kill weeds between stones and bricks, or where children and pets play, pour a boiling hot solution of 1 oz. liquid dish soap and 1 oz. gin in a quart of water over the area.

TIP #3

To make an old fashioned rain barrel, buy a 30 gallon plastic garbage can, cut a small hole in the lid, and place it under a down spout with the spout through the hole. Then insert a cheap plastic spigot near the bottom of the can.

TIP #4

For a great late summer snack for your lawn, mix all of the left-over lawn, garden and flower food you have laying around, and apply it with your hand-held spreader set on the medium setting.

✕ AROUND THE YARD

TIP #5

To get a bed border that's perfectly edged, cut through
the sod using an up-and-down sawing motion with
a sharp carving knife, using a strip of wood or
plastic as a guide the way you would use a
ruler to draw a straight line.

TIP #6

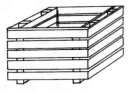

Discarded shipping pallets make great com-
post bins. Place one pallet on the ground, and
drive 2 metal support poles per side into the
ground. Then slip the pallet sides over top of
the poles and your bin is complete.

TIP #7

Whether you are landscaping on a
large scale or just adding a few plants,
take a photograph of your outdoor
green scene and keep it in a scrap-
book, labeled with the plant names,
where purchased (save the receipts

also), when purchased, where they are planted and some care
tips. If you're ordering plants from a catalog, cut out the pictures
and information. This way, you always have all your plant information at hand.

TIP #8

How you spray does make a difference! With a compressed air
sprayer you can put the right spray...right on target...in the right
amount. It's easy to spray under the leaves, too!

TIP #9

A small extension curtain rod makes a good support for tall plants. As the plants grow, the rod can be adjusted so that it is always the right height.

TIP #10

To untie knots in rope, twine, ribbon, or string that you're using to hold up your plants, sprinkle baby powder or talcum powder on them.

TIP #11

To increase the organic activity in your soil, add 1 tbsp. of regular (non-diet) cola to your plant food mix. You might just say that things grow better with Coke®.

TIP #12

Pantyhose make the best ties. Simply cut the legs of panty hose diagonally in 1-1/2" pieces, and wear them on your wrist. Then weave as many pieces together for the length of tie needed. The top of pantyhose can also be used on a pail as a strainer.

TIP #13

Wash your hands, wrists and ankles with a heavy lather of Fels Naptha soap after gardening. This will help take the sting out of Poison Ivy and bug bites.

TREES,
Shrubs & Evergreens

TIP #14

Don't spare the rod when it comes to your trees! Striking a tree trunk with a stick or rolled up newspaper stimulates sap flow in early spring.

TIP #15

Nip pests early! Stop over-wintering insects by applying dormant spray (a mixture of lime sulphur and Volck Oil) to deciduous trees and woody plants before the buds open.

TIP #16

Exercise your evergreens to keep them growing tall, full, and wide. Shake them gently from time to time to get rid of the dandruff and older needles.

TIP #17

Leave no leaf unsprayed! To get rid of pests, spray plants thoroughly-especially under leaves where most disease starts and many bugs hide.

TIP #18

Evergreens were "ever lucky" in early New England. A pair of evergreens were planted in the dooryard of newlyweds to symbolize health and long life.

TIP #19

To properly water your evergreens, bury PVC tubing, 4"-5" in diameter and 10" long, between them, and fill the tubing with rocks. The top of the tubing should be 1" below ground level. Water directly into the tubing.

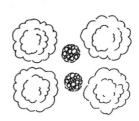

TIP #20

To help water your trees, place flexible irrigation pipe in the bottom of the hole when planting, fill the pipe with rocks, and plant the tree on top of it. Water directly into the pipe. The tree roots will grow around this root watering system.

TIP #21

To help your sick trees, wrap them with 4" wide strips of burlap from the ground up to the first branch. Leave the tree wrapped through the hot weather. This wrap acts as insulation, keeping the tree cool and moist.

America's Master Gardener®

♣ TREES, SHRUBS & EVERGREENS

TIP #22

If you have to use decorative stone, first place a layer of landscape fabric around your trees, shrubs, and evergreens. Cover with 2" of dried, brown grass clippings. Then place decorative stone on top of the grass clippings. The grass clippings absorb the heat from the stones, and the landscape fabric helps prevent weeds.

TIP #23

To get rid of bugs, cut a piece of burlap 10" wide and long enough to wrap around the tree trunk so that it overlaps by 2". Spray one side with TangleTrap or other sticky substance. Wrap the burlap around the top of the trunk, sticky side out. Secure to the tree by tying a nylon stocking around the center of the burlap. Allow the top half to drape down over the bottom half. As bugs climb up the trunk, they will get trapped in between the two sticky surfaces and die.

TIP #24

When pruning, close all tree wounds with expandable foam (like Great-Stuff®) to prevent borers.

TIP #25

In fall, secure young trees with a taut rope through
a garden hose which is pulled back into the
prevailing winter wind. Release them in spring.

TIP #26

To use a milk jug as a watering can, put 5 or 6 tiny nail holes in the
bottom, fill with water, and place it at the base of each tree. There
is no standing there for long periods, waiting for the water to soak
in; just fill the jug and walk away. The water will soak in slowly
with no run-off.

TIP #27

Your fruit and nut tree branches are good for outdoor cooking. Cut
the larger branches into 6 to 8" lengths. They burn down nicely to
form a bed of coals for barbecuing. Smaller twigs make a great
bed for kindling, and can be used to smoke meats. The wood
imparts a delicious flavor to grilled food, and the wood ash by-
product can be added to your garden as well.

TIP #28

A simple, inexpensive wooden guide rail makes
hedge trimming fast, easy, and accurate.

FLOWERS

TIP #29

Hammer away at the ends of the stems of fresh cut flowers and branches of flowering shrubs before placing them in a vase. This allows them to quickly draw up water.

TIP #30

Gesundheit! Make sure you give annuals a soaking...but not a cold! Aim at their toes, not their nose. And don't sprinkle their clothes.

TIP #31

Learn to tell bulbs' noses from their basal plates, and plant them heads up!

TIP #32

Add a tablespoon of charcoal in the bottom of a flower vase to prolong the life of cut flowers.

TIP #33

Inexpensive flower holders can be made of galvanized wire netting (hardware cloth) cut to fit the bowl where they will be used. Bend the four corners of each piece to form legs about an inch high.

TIP #34

Don't use scented flowers at the dinner table. Heavily scented flowers such as gardenias, hyacinths, etc., shouldn't be used for table decorations because the strong perfume in a hot room frequently spoils the appetite.

✿✿✿ FLOWERS

TIP #35

To restore faded flowers, immerse them half
way up their stems in very hot water, and allow
them to remain in it until it cools. Then cut off
the scalded portions of the stems, and place
the flowers in clear, cold water.

TIP #36

To help your summer flowering bulbs survive
the winter, dust them with medicated baby
powder before storing them in old onion
sacks for the winter.

TIP #37

To hold blossoms longer, spray cut
flowers with hairspray.

TIP #38

To dye white carnations, cut the stems and place them in hot water with food coloring added. Let them set for one hour.

TIP #39

Picking flowers frequently encourages most annuals to flower more abundantly.

TIP #40

If you want a straight-edged perennial bed, simply drive small stakes in at the corners and stretch a string between them. For a curved edge, mark the shape you want with your garden hose.

⚵⚵ FLOWERS

TIP #41

Save your old umbrellas because the ribs make excellent, long-lasting supports for flowers. Paint them green, and they will hardly be seen in your garden.

TIP #42

Remove dead flowers from annual and perennial bedding plants. Possible sites of infection are removed along with the dead tissues, and the plants' energy is directed to further flower production. Spike flowers like delphiniums should not be cut off right to the ground, since lateral growth will develop from below, and flower later.

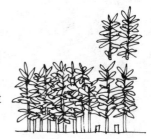

TIP #43

Trailing plants like dwarf phlox and various moss pinks are cut back after flowering to retain their compact habit. This treatment may encourage a second crop of flowers from your bedding plants.

TIP #44

Garlic to the rescue: if you put 1 or 2 garlic cloves into your rose bushes, they will never be bothered by aphids or other insects.

TIP #45

FOR CLUMPS
OF BULBS
DIG 6" DEEP
TRENCH

When your spring flowering bulbs are in full bloom, take pictures of them or make a diagram of where they are for 2 reasons: first, it'll help you decide where you need more of the same, or a different color, next year, and second, you'll know right where the bulbs are so you don't damage them when planting more bulbs this fall.

TIP #46

You can remove the faded flowers from bulbs, but the foliage must be left on to provide the bulb with food for next year's flowers.

ꗽꗽꗽ FLOWERS

TIP #47

Instead of cutting the foliage off of bulbs,
give it a neater appearance by folding it
in half, and holding it in place with elas-
tic or a rubberband.

TIP #48

If you've naturalized bulbs in your lawn, don't cut the foliage or the
bulbs will deteriorate rapidly.

TIP #49

The best way of marking dahlias is to use tongue depressors
marked with a wood burning tool. Burn the name of the dahlia on
one side, and the color and type on the other. Drill a small hole in
the top of the stick, tie a string to it at planting time, and then retie
the stick to the tuber at storing time.

VEGETABLES

TIP #50

To make a great water bubbler for
watering your vegetable garden,
place one old sock inside another
old sock, and then place a piece of

brick in the toe. Now wire the socks to the end of a garden hose,
and use it in your vegetable garden.

TIP #51

Yesterday's news makes an excellent
garden mulch. Put down up to 3
alternating layers of single newspaper sheets, and then lay 3 inches
of grass clippings over top.

TIP #52

Keep birds out of your garden by hanging tin
can lids by strawberry or other fruit plants.

VEGETABLES

TIP #53

To water your vegetable garden, bury cans, with both ends removed, between your vegetable plants. Fill the cans with rocks. Water directly into the cans; the water will run through to the roots.

TIP #54

Old hangers make great plant markers. Simply cut a long piece of hanger, wrap it around a 2" piece of pipe twice, slice it off, and then press together. Now, insert plastic cards or seed packs into the slot.

TIP #55

To start up to 12 plants at a time, use a clean egg carton as a seed starter container. Punch holes in the bottom of each section for drainage, and fill with professional potting mix.

TIP #56

To protect seedlings from the weather and varmints, cut the bottom or side out of a 1 gallon milk carton, and place it over the tender young plants.

TIP #57

To avoid cutworm damage to your plants, wrap a strip of newspaper 2 or 3 times around the seedling stems at planting level.

TIP #58

If you use milk jugs on your vegetables or flowers in spring for mini-hothouses, instead of cutting the bottom completely off, leave one side attached. Fold the bottom back, place over the plant, and put a rock or some dirt on the folded back bottom. This keeps them from blowing away.

TIP #59

To help you find where you planted your carrots, mix radish seeds in with them to mark the rows. Radishes sprout faster than carrots, so you will know where you planted your carrots much sooner.

America's / Master Gardener®

HOUSE PLANTS

TIP #60

A layer of granulated charcoal on top of potting soil filters out any unwanted additives in the water.

GRANULATED CHARCOAL

TIP #61

You can make a vacation hothouse for your house plants by loosely draping a plastic dry cleaning bag over a coathanger frame. This will retain soil moisture for up to 2 weeks.

TIP #62

For no-mess watering of your hanging plants, let a few ice cubes slowly melt into the soil.

TIP #63

You're sure to have success with wax begonias indoors if you plant them in clay pots, and keep them in a western exposure. The late afternoon winter sun seems to do wonders for them. And they are easier to water if you line up the clay pots on a plastic tray.

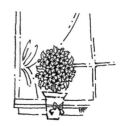

TIP #64

Eggshells are a great source of calcium for your plants. Dry them in the oven or microwave, crush them as fine as possible, and then add them to the planter mix or soil.

TIP #65

A dose of castor oil saves ferns: add 1 tbsp. castor oil and 1 tbsp. children's shampoo to a quart of warm water, and give each plant a 1/4 cup of the mixture.

🌺 HOUSE PLANTS

TIP #66

Bricks can save your plants' lives. When you go on vacation, place a plant on a brick in an old bucket and cover the brick with water; it will last for a couple of weeks.

TIP #67

Keep a pan of water close to the radiator in a room where house plants are growing. It will help moisten the atmosphere which is necessary if you want the plants to thrive.

TIP #68

Watch the soil of small plants! Many small plants are lost because the surface of the soil becomes hard, crusted, and compacted, and the little seedlings do not have sufficient strength to force their way through. Add 1 tsp. children's shampoo per quart of warm water or plant food mixture to keep the soil soft.

TIP #69

Always mix your plant food with very warm water because plants will take it up faster.

TIP #70

Place a moth ball on the soil of all house plants that are outdoors one month before you bring them in to help get rid of any pests that have taken up residence.

TIP #71

To circulate the air in a room full of plants, hide a small oscillating fan on top of a high cabinet, and plug it into a timer so that it automatically goes on and off at selected times. It will also help hold down your heat bill.

❦ HOUSE PLANTS

TIP #72

You can make inexpensive plant pots from decorated plastic butter, cottage cheese or topping containers. Clean them thoroughly before using, and poke small holes in the bottom for drainage.

TIP #73

A cedar stake the size of a pencil placed in the soil of your house plants will discourage soil insects.

TIP #74

When repotting your house plants, mix a cup of fireplace ashes with 2 quarts of potting soil to strengthen the stems and foliage.

TIP #75

Waterproof the sides of clay pots by spraying them with two coats of ScotchGuard® from the top down to 1" above the bottom of the pot.

TIP #76

Place egg shells in the microwave for three minutes, remove, crush into a fine powder, and place them in a cloth sachet. Then drop the sachet into your house plant watering can.

TIP #77

To prevent water damage and mud spots on your carpet, always place a good size plant underneath your hanging plants. That way, any drips or spills will be caught by the plant on the floor.

🌹 HOUSE PLANTS

TIP #78

A chicken wire dome, with a small opening in the top, placed over a potted vine type plant will keep the center open for water and air.

TIP #79

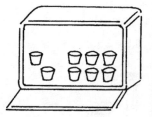

If you take little paper cups, fill them with my house plant tonic, and place them in the freezer, you now have a handy way to water hanging baskets.

TIP #80

To keep bugs out of the soil of your house plants, simply sprinkle pencil sharpening shavings on top of the soil.

TIP #81

Torn leaves on your house plants can be mended with clear nail polish applied to both sides of the leaf.

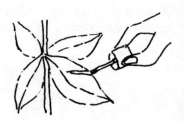

TIP #82

The fumes from new stain resistant carpeting can be death to your plants. So either put up with the old carpet or put your plants outside or in another room for about a year after recarpeting.

TIP #83

Recycle those foam packing "peanuts" by using them in the bottom of your clay pots when repotting. They are lighter than pieces of clay, and are particularly good for hanging plants.

TIP #84

Print the various formulas you use to water your house plants on index cards. On the back of each card, write in the date you use that tonic so you don't use the same one each time.

TIP #85

The best indoor insect repellent for house plants is pieces of moth ball crystals applied directly to the surface of the soil.

PETS, PESTS
& Other Critters

TIP #86

Hit the bug's eye! For on-target spraying, use a sprayer that has a spray extension and adjustable nozzle.

TIP #87

To kill snails and slugs, fill an old pie tin with beer and 3 drops of vinegar, and bury it at ground level. The little critters will drown themselves.

TIP #88

To introduce toads to your garden, set out toad houses - clay pots turned upside down with a hole broken out for a door. Place the pot in the shade, and provide a shallow pan of water.

TIP #89

Nothing keeps varmints away like a cat. So pamper your favorite feline by planting a small patch of catnip in your garden. It will certainly become a favorite napping site.

TIP #90

To keep cats and squirrels from climbing trees, place a 12" wide piece of sheet metal around the trunk, 6' to 7' off the ground.

TIP #91

When using chicken wire to prevent rabbit damage to tree trunks, place 4 sticks (the diameter of your little finger) between the tree and the chicken wire. This prevents the rabbits from getting to the bark.

PETS, PESTS & OTHER CRITTERS

TIP #92

Hardware cloth is best to keep mice from girding the bark of young trees (wrap the trunk with tree wrap first). And be sure to sprinkle Repel® into all winter mulch.

TIP #93

The best mouse trap bait is pumpkin seeds; you'll find that mice can't resist them.

TIP #94

Trying to trap raccoons? Use marshmallows as bait. Place 1 in a trap, and small pieces of another leading to the trap door. The raccoon's sweet tooth will do the rest.

TIP #95

Many pests hide in a shady place during the day. Set a trap by laying a board on a damp part of your garden in early evening. Come morning, lift it up and crush the thugs with your shoe or drown them in a pail of water.

TIP #96

Try using a mixture of coffee grounds and cut up orange peels scattered around your favorite plants to keep cats from using your garden as a litter box.

TIP #97

To make a codling moth trap for your apple trees, take a plastic gallon milk jug, and in one of the panels opposite the handle, cut an opening large enough to reach inside. Mix equal parts of vinegar and water, and pour the solution into the bottom of the jug until it is 1" deep. Add a few tablespoons of black-strap molasses. Hang 1 trap in each small tree. Larger trees may need 2 or more jugs. Space them about 6' apart. Check the traps weekly, and remove the trapped moths.

PETS, PESTS & OTHER CRITTERS

TIP #98

If you want to keep deer, groundhogs, and other varmints out of your corn patch, get some human hair clippings and place them on the corn blade next to the stalk. The human odor keeps them away.

TIP #99

To keep the birds away from your crops, cut black plastic garbage bags into strips about 2" to 3" wide, 3' long, and tie them in a cherry tree or place them in the strawberry patch.

TIP #100

If you want to catch moths and black bugs on your raspberries, add 1 cup sugar, 1/2 cup vinegar, and 1 banana peel to a gallon milk jug filled with water about 2" from the top. Set it among your raspberry bushes, and leave it in place all summer. You can also divide the mixture and put it in soda cans.

TIP #101

To get rid of peach tree worms, stir 1 cup vinegar and 1 cup sugar into 1 quart of warm water. Fill a quart-size jar with the mixture, and hang it from a peach tree when it is in full bloom. One quart of this tonic is enough to attract all insects that produce worms in a medium-sized peach orchard.